CONTENTS

Chapter 1

HOW DO YOU TRAVEL?   4–7
Which Way to Travel   6

Chapter 2

SHORT JOURNEYS   8-17
Using Public Transport   10
Travel by Bus or Train   13
Using a Car   14
Shopping Trips   17

Chapter 3

TRANSPORT AND POLLUTION   18-21
Less Fuel, Less Pollution   20

Chapter 4

LONGER JOURNEYS   23-25
Going by Plane   24

Chapter 5

TOO MUCH TRAFFIC   26-29
Easing the Load   28

Transport Topic Web   30

Glossary   31
Further Reading   31
Index   32

How do you Travel?

There are many different ways of travelling from one place to another. You might walk to school from home, but travel by bus or by car when you go shopping.

When you go on holiday, you may go by train or by boat. Or you may fly in an aeroplane. Trams, bicycles, cars, buses, trains are all different means of transport.

Japanese students walk across a road on their way to college. The students are wearing uniforms and carrying bags full of books.

Transport

ANGELA ROYSTON

HODDER
Wayland

Environment Starts Here!
Transport

OTHER TITLES IN THE SERIES
Food · Water · Recycling

Produced for Wayland Publishers Limited by
Lionheart Books
10, Chelmsford Square
London NW10 3AR
England

Designer: Ben White

Editor: Lionel Bender

Picture Research: Madeleine Samuel

Electronic make-up: Mike Pilley, Radius

Illustrated by Rudi Visi

First Published in Great Britain in 1998 by Wayland (Publishers) Ltd
Reprinted in 2001 by Hodder Wayland,
an imprint of Hodder Children's Books

© Hodder Wayland 1998

British Library Cataloguing in Publication Data
Royston, Angela
Transport. - (Environment starts here! ; 4)
1. Transportation - Environmental aspects - Juvenile literature
I. Title
388
ISBN 0 7502 3490 3

Printed and bound in Hong Kong
Picture Acknowledgements
Pages 1: Zefa/Stockmarket/Starfoto. 4: Eye Ubiquitous/John Dakers. 5: Britstock-IFA/
F. Aberham. 6: Ecoscene/Martin Jones. 8: Zefa/Stockmarket. 9: Zefa/Stockmarket/Strange.
10, 11: Zefa/Stockmarket. 12: Eye Ubiquitous/G. Daniels. 14: Britstock/IFA/West Stock.
17: Ecoscene/Mike Maidment. 18: Ecoscene/Amanda Gasidis. 19: Britstock-IFA/Jim Pickerell.
20: Ole Steen Hensen. 21: Britstock/IFA/Jay. 22: Zefa/Stockmarket. 23: Ecoscene/Stephen
Coyne. 24: Zefa/Stockmarket/Damm. 25: Eye Ubiquitous/Craig Hutchins. 26: Wayland Photo
Library/V. Wright. 27: Zefa/Stockmarket/Sunak. 29: Wayland Photo Library/Christine
Osborne. Cover: Zefa Photo Library/Stockmarket.

The photo on page 1 shows traffic-filled streets in New Delhi, India.

A ferryboat packed with cars, trucks, coaches and passengers leaves a harbour. More vehicles are lined up, waiting to board the next boat.

5

Which Way to Travel

The best way to travel depends on how far you are going, what you are carrying, the weather and how much it will cost.

In this city street in England, children walk across the road, while other people use a bicycle, coach, van and cars for transport.

On the move

Think about your last school holidays. Make a list of the forms of transport mentioned on these two pages and write down how many times you used each one. Which one did you use most often? Why do you think that was so?

A comparison of journey times

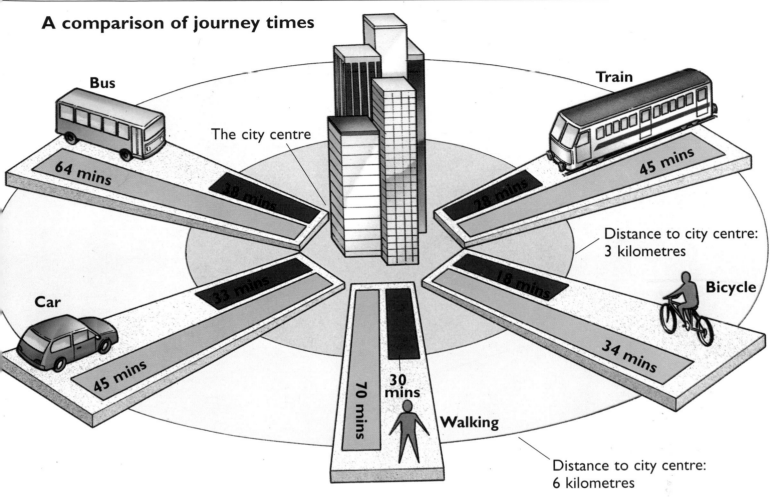

Bus — 64 mins — 38 mins

The city centre

Train — 45 mins — 28 mins

Distance to city centre: 3 kilometres

Bicycle — 34 mins — 18 mins

Car — 45 mins — 33 mins

Walking — 70 mins — 30 mins

Distance to city centre: 6 kilometres

For short distances, walking and cycling are the cheapest types of transport. In city centres, they are also often the fastest. For longer distances, a train, coach or plane may be fastest.

Whatever your journey, if you have a lot of things to carry and many places to visit, a car may be the most useful type of transport.

This diagram shows the journey times to a city centre using different types of transport. Since there is lots of traffic in city centres, walking is usually faster.

Short Journeys

These adults in Beijing, the capital city of China, are travelling by bicycle. When cycling on main roads, it is safest to wear a helmet.

Do you sometimes cycle to your friend's house? It's faster than walking! Many adults cycle to work because the exercise is good for their health. Also, cycling is quick and cheap, and it does not cause pollution.

Cycling is not always the best type of transport because you cannot carry many things on a bike, and if it rains, you get wet.

A monorail train carries passengers above the streets in the city of Sydney in Australia.

Using Public Transport

Buses, trains and trams are called public transport because anyone can use them, provided they buy a ticket.

Public transport is convenient if you have a lot to carry, or if you are going farther than you can walk. People can travel together, right into the centre of a town or city, and they do not have to find a place to park.

Most passengers sit, but a few stand, inside this carriage of a city train in Singapore.

City transport

In a major city, types of public transport include buses, trains and trams. Some trains run underground.

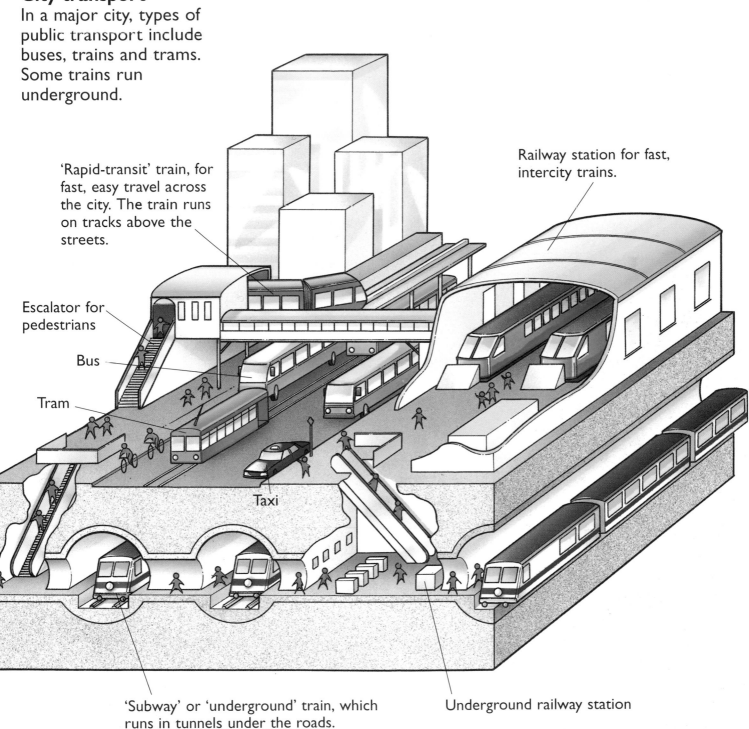

'Rapid-transit' train, for fast, easy travel across the city. The train runs on tracks above the streets.

Railway station for fast, intercity trains.

Escalator for pedestrians

Bus

Tram

Taxi

'Subway' or 'underground' train, which runs in tunnels under the roads.

Underground railway station

Passengers leaving a train at a railway station. Many of the passengers are travelling with suitcases and other luggage.

12

Travel by Bus or Train

Public transport helps everyone. If fewer people travel by car, there are fewer traffic jams and road accidents. Also, the air is less polluted by exhaust fumes.

Buses, trains and trams keep to set routes, so you may have to take more than one type of public transport to get somewhere.

In the town of Thuringen in Germany, buses run alongside trams, taking passengers from the main railway station.

Using a Car

People often use a car to travel to work, or to visit friends and relatives. Some parents take their children to school by car on their way to work.

Travelling by car is comfortable and convenient. You can travel from door to door, and keep warm and dry, even in bad weather. And you do not have to worry about buying tickets or reserving a seat for the journey.

A family packs bags and equipment into the boot of their car, ready to go on holiday.

Comparing types of transport

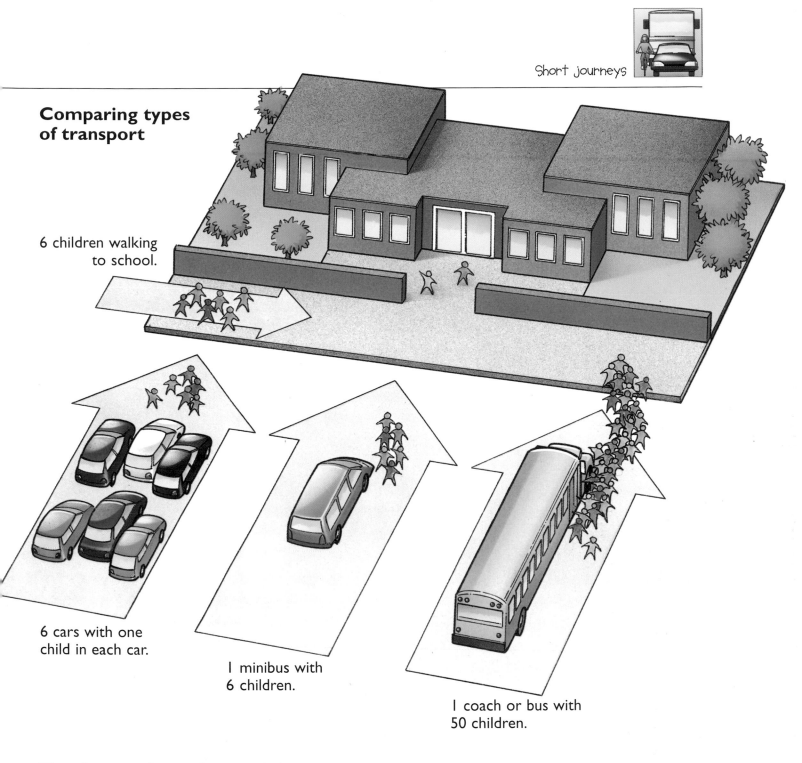

6 children walking to school.

6 cars with one child in each car.

1 minibus with 6 children.

1 coach or bus with 50 children.

This diagram shows that a coach can carry many more passengers than several cars. If more coaches are used, there is less traffic on the roads.

Shopping centre transport

Roads leading to and from
shopping centres allow
trucks to deliver goods
and shoppers to arrive by
car or bus.

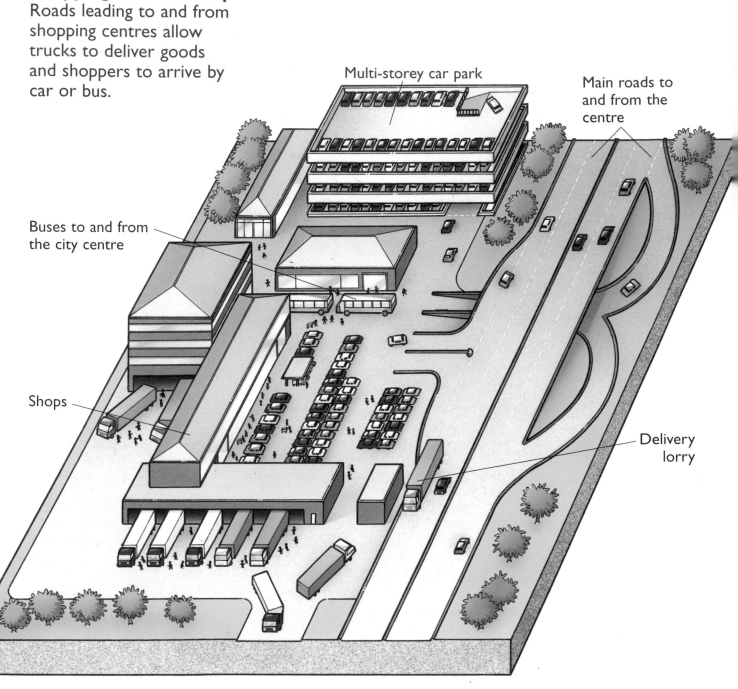

Multi-storey car park

Main roads to
and from the
centre

Buses to and from
the city centre

Shops

Delivery
lorry

Shopping Trips

Supermarkets and shopping centres have large car parks attached. The whole family can shop together and carry everything home in the car.

Large shopping centres on the edge of towns often include a petrol station, places to eat and play areas for children. Some people think that out-of-town shopping centres make people use their cars too much, causing traffic jams.

A woman loads bags from her supermarket shopping trolley into the boot of her car to take home.

Transport and Pollution

Buses, cars and other forms of transport that burn petrol or diesel oil produce waste gases, which pollute, or poison, the air. These 'exhaust fumes' can make people feel ill, or make it difficult for them to breathe.

Exhaust fumes also pollute the water in clouds with harmful chemicals. Rain from the clouds damages brickwork and stonework on buildings, and kills fish in rivers and lakes.

In heavy town traffic, a cyclist wears a face mask to avoid breathing in harmful fumes from vehicles.

Fumes from cars on a motorway in the USA create a 'fog' in the air.

19

Less Fuel, Less Pollution

Modern vehicles use less fuel than old ones. They are also fitted with special pipes that clean exhaust fumes before they enter the air.

Electric vehicles do not produce exhaust fumes and for short journeys often cost less to run than petrol and diesel vehicles. But power stations that make electricity burn coal, oil and gas, causing pollution.

A man fills his car with unleaded petrol, which contains less harmful chemicals than ordinary engine fuels.

A double-decked tram in Hong Kong is powered by electricity through overhead cables and poles.

Yellow taxi cabs fill this street in New York City in the USA. Travelling by taxi avoids having to park the car or wait for a bus or tram, but it can be expensive.

Longer Journeys

For long journeys, people travel by train, coach, car, boat or plane. Trains and coaches are ideal for groups of people with luggage who want to travel together.

Travelling long distances by car is convenient, but going by train or plane is often quicker and easier. To cross large lakes and seas, travelling by boat or plane are the only choices.

Passengers and cars unload from a ferryboat in Greece.

Going by Plane

To go really long distances, by far the best means of transport is to fly in an aeroplane. A plane can cover thousands of kilometres in just a few hours. But there are problems with planes.

An aeroplane uses a huge amount of fuel which pollutes the air. Travelling by plane is expensive. You also have to spend several hours travelling to the airport and waiting for the plane to load and refuel.

Passengers at Frankfurt Airport in Germany look for the check-in desks for their international flights.

A plane takes off from an airport. Planes are very noisy, so they disturb people who live near airports.

Too much Traffic

The streets in towns and cities are often clogged with cars and trucks. The traffic has to move very slowly and the slightest problem causes a traffic jam.

A teacher helps children to board a school bus in the USA. The children enjoy travelling together, and their parents do not have to use their cars for school journeys.

Traffic jams slow down travellers and cause extra pollution as vehicles wait with their engines running. If fire engines and ambulances are held up, the delay can make the difference between life and death.

Pedestrians and many kinds of transport fill these streets in the city of Lucknow in northern India.

Easing the Load

Most towns and cities now make it difficult for car drivers to park in city centres. They provide car parks on the edge of the town or city, close to trains and buses.

Less Traffic

What can your family do to help cut down traffic pollution and traffic jams? Here are some ideas:

• Walk to school and to friends who live nearby.
• Use your local shops.
• Do not drive into the city or town centre.
• Go by bus or train instead of by car whenever possible.

Can you think of other ways of cutting down traffic?

In many cities, some major roads are marked with special lanes for public transport vehicles, emergency vehicles and bicycles.

Park-and-ride bus. This takes passengers to and from an out-of-town car park and the city centre.

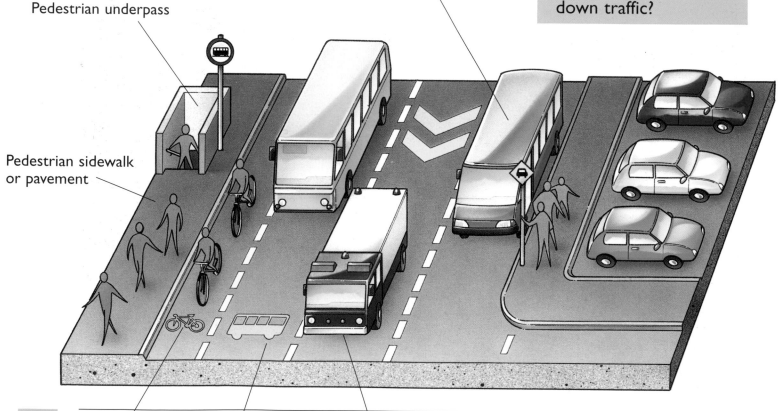

Pedestrian underpass

Pedestrian sidewalk or pavement

Bicycle lane

Bus lane

Emergency vehicle lane

Special bus lanes help buses avoid traffic jams, and cycle paths alongside roads make cycling safer. Many town centres keep traffic out altogether and allow only cyclists and pedestrians to use the streets.

Trams like this one, in Amsterdam, the Netherlands, help reduce the number of cars in city centres.

Transport Topic Web

Maths
Measuring diameter, circumference, radius of a circle.
Data handling.
Modes of transport used for getting to school.
Car colours, shapes, sizes.

Using a trundle wheel to measure the classroom and playground.
Counting in 2s (motorbike or bicycle wheels).
Counting in 4s (car wheels).

Geography
Compass points, N, S, E, W.
Planning a journey.
Collections of maps, tickets, and so on.
Model road layout – road safety.

P.E./Dance Drama
Moving like different vehicles.
Direction games.

IT
Programme a turtle or pixie – changing directions.

ART
Paintings with car wheels.
Photographs.
Look at famous paintings involving transport, for example, Van Gogh, Constable.

Music
Singing songs with transport as a theme, for example, *Michael row the boat ashore*.
Use of musical instruments to create engine sounds.

Transport

Technology
Design and make a 'buggy'.
Design and make a boat that floats.

R.E.
Pilgrimages and significant journeys.
What special journeys have children made? What made them special?

Language
Read stories/poems with transport as a theme, for example, John Burningham's *Mr Gumpy's Motorcar*.
Acrostic poems.
Writing instructions for a journey.

History
Old/new – changing features of different modes of transport.
Timeline – the motor car, aeroplanes, and so on, when they were invented and milestones in development.
Historic journeys?

Science
Do wheels have to be round? Make different shaped wheels.
Do they roll?
Friction – brakes, slowing down, stopping.
Moving a heavy load – for example, by using rollers, pulling.
Which is easiest?

Glossary

Bus lane Part of the road which only buses, and perhaps taxis and bicycles, are allowed to use.

Diesel oil A fuel used by buses, trucks, some trains and some cars.

Environment Everything in the surroundings, such as air, land and water.

Exhaust fumes Waste gases given off by vehicles which burn oil or petrol. Some of these gases poison the air and alter the Earth's climate.

Fossil fuel Fuels such as oil, coal and gas which take millions of years to form under the ground.

Fuel Something which is burned to produce energy. Vehicles burn fuel to produce energy which is turned into movement.

Passenger Someone who travels in a vehicle, but does not drive it.

Pedestrian A person who walks.

Pollute To allow dirty or harmful waste to escape into the air, or into water or onto the land.

Public transport A vehicle such as a bus, train, plane or tram, which charges a fare and carries many passengers along a set route.

Traffic jam Vehicles brought to a standstill because the road is blocked or filled with too many vehicles for the width of the road.

Transport Any vehicle or way of travelling from one place to another.

Further Reading

Cars, Planes, Ships and Trains by Ian Graham (Heinemann 1996).

People and Journeys by Rosemary Rees and Janet Withersby (Heinemann 1996).

The Green Detective On The Road by John Baines (Wayland, 1992).

Transport Around the World by Godfrey Hall (Wayland, 1995).

World About Us: Traffic Pollution by Michael Bright (Gloucester Press, 1991).

Worldwise Cars by Scott Steadman (Watts Books, 1995).

Index

Airports 25

Bicycles and cycling 4, 6, 8, 18, 28, 29

Boats 4, 23

Buses 4, 10, 13, 18, 26, 28, 29, 31

Cars 4, 5, 6, 7, 14, 15, 18, 22, 26, 28, 31

Car parks 16, 17, 28

Carrying 4, 8, 10, 17

Cities 7, 8, 9, 10, 22, 24, 27, 28

Coaches 6, 15, 23

Costs 6, 7, 22, 24

Distances 7, 8

Exhaust fumes 13, 18, 19, 20, 31

Ferryboats 5, 23

Fuel 20, 24, 31

Holidays 4, 6, 14

Journey times 7, 8, 24

Motorway 19

Park-and-ride 28

Passengers 12, 13, 15, 23, 29, 31

Pedestrians 11, 27, 28, 29, 31

Planes 7, 23, 24, 25

Pollution 8, 13, 18, 20, 24, 26, 28, 31

Public transport 10, 11, 13, 28, 31

Safety 8

Shopping trips 4, 8, 16, 17, 28

Speeds 7

Stations 11, 12, 13

Taxi cabs 22

Traffic 13, 18, 26, 28, 29, 31

Trains 4, 7, 9, 10, 11, 12, 13, 23, 28

Trams 4, 10, 13, 21, 29

Trucks and vans 5, 6, 26

Walking 4, 8